YOUR KNOWLEDGE HAS VALUE

Max Sahle

Initial conditions, policies and growth in the former Soviet bloc

What have we learned so far and implications for the future

GRIN Verlag

Bibliografische Information der Deutschen Nationalbibliothek:

Die Deutsche Bibliothek verzeichnet diese Publikation in der Deutschen National-
bibliografie; detaillierte bibliografische Daten sind im Internet über http://dnb.d-
nb.de/ abrufbar.

Imprint:

Copyright © 2013 GRIN Verlag GmbH
Druck und Bindung: Books on Demand GmbH, Norderstedt Germany
ISBN: 978-3-656-76231-7

This book at GRIN:

http://www.grin.com/en/e-book/281611/initial-conditions-policies-and-growth-in-
the-former-soviet-bloc

Initial conditions, policies and growth in the countries of the former Soviet bloc:

What have we learned so far and implications for the future.

Contents

Introduction

By the late 1980s, the ever more apparent failures and shortcomings of the planned economy and the collapse of the Communist political system in almost all countries of the Soviet Block enabled dramatic changes to all parts of society and the economy. Since the market economies of Western Europe and North America were the obvious reference point, transforming the planned economies into functioning market economies became a priority. This transition would ensure a better allocation of resources as well as technological progress and innovation and foster sustainable economic growth. To achieve this, it was necessary to profoundly change the underlying structures and incentives of the planned economy. While each country embarked on its own path towards a market economy, there is little dispute as to what reforms were necessary to get the new economic system going. Following Hare these include: (1) macroeconomic stabilisation; (2) price and trade liberalization; (3) privatization and enterprise restructuring; and (4) institutional reforms.[1]

This essay examines the impact of some of these reforms on growth. It will also look into how initial conditions explain differences in growth outcomes that can't be fully explained by policy choices. Focusing on inflation and fiscal balances, the first section will explore the role of macroeconomic stabilization in fostering growth. This is followed by section 2 and 3 which examine institutional reforms and liberalization. Section 5 takes a look at initial conditions in the form of overall development and economic distortions at the start of the transition period. Section 6 concludes and draws implications for the future.

Macroeconomic stabilisation and growth

There appears to be a broad consensus in the literature that achieving macroeconomic stabilization is essential for economic growth. Macroeconomic stability is usually measured by the inflation rate and fiscal deficits. Its absence complicates planning and discourages saving and investment. Inflation rates in the early 1990s were as high as 4500% dropping to an average of 7% in 2007 in the transition countries as transition progressed and stabilization was achieved.[2] The significance of stabilisation is made clear by a paper by Havrylyshyn and Rooden in which they find that macroeconomic stability, measured by inflation rates and fiscal deficits is highly significant in explaining economic growth and accounts for up to 90% of the variation in growth across the region.[3] Their results are supported by

---

[1]Hare, 'Institutions in transition', in P. G Hare and Gerard Turley(ed.), Handbook of the Economics and Political Economy of Transition, London and New York, Routledge, 2013, pp. 34-46 (p. 34)

[2]   Ibid., pp.18-19

[3]Havrylyshyn and van Rooden, 'Institutions Matter in Transiton, But so do Policies', Comaparative Economic Studies, 45, 2003, pp. 2-24 (p. 14)

Gerry, Lee and Mickiewicz whose estimations show a consistently negative impact of higher inflation on growth.[4] Similarly Hare finds that higher inflation and larger deficits are associated with deeper recessions at the outset of the transition process in 1992 to 1994.[5]Falcetti, Lysenko and Sanfey's estimations find comparable results for fiscal balances, arguing that a large fiscal deficit leads to lower growth rates.[6] This is also supported by findings from the European Bank for Reconstruction and Development (EBRD). These show a negative impact of fiscal deficits and an especially big impact in the early transition years.[7]

Realizing that high inflation is bad for growth naturally raises the question how far inflation rates should be reduced. There are studies finding that the relationship between inflation and growth is nonlinear and that, once inflation is below a certain threshold it does no more harm. There is however no consensus as to where this threshold is. Christoffersen and Doyle find that inflation rates above 13-15% can reduce output growth by 0.2%. They state the examples of Armenia and Russia which have reduced their inflation rates by 9 and 7 times, thus increasing growth by 1.8% and 1.4% respectively. However, their findings also suggest that increasing inflation if it is below the threshold does not benefit growth.[8] Reviewing the literature, Falcetti, Lysenko and Sanfey put the threshold at 10-20% and citing (Loungani and Sheets (1997)) find that an inflation rate above 500% leads to a decline in economic growth by 2% in the following year and a loss of 4% over the long run.[9] Yet another threshold is found by Fischer, Sahay and Vegh at 50%[10] and the EBRD in its 1999 transition report puts it at 30%. They also support the notion that reducing inflation if it

[4]Gerry, Lee and Mickiewicz, 'Governance, Institutions and Growth: empirical lessons from the post-communist transition', in Enrico Marelli and Marcello Signorelli (ed.),
Economic Growth and Structural Features of Transition, United Kingdom, Palgrave Macmillian, 2010, pp. 41-60 (pp. 44-45, 55)

[5]Hare, 'Institutions in transition', in P. G Hare and Gerard Turley(ed.), Handbook of the Economics and Political Economy of Transition, London and New York, Routledge, 2013, pp. 34-46 (p. 41)

[6]Falcetti, Lysenko and Sanfey, 'Reforms and growth in transition: re-examining the evidence', EBRD Working Paper, 90, 2005, pp.1-26 (p.12)

[7]European Bank for Reconstruction and Development, 'Transition Report 2008: Growth in Transition', EBRD Transition Report, 2008, pp.1-224 (p. 2)

[8] Christoffersen and Doyle, 'From Inflation to Growth: eight years of transition', Economics of Transition, 8 (2), 2000, pp. 421-451 (pp. 435-437)

[9]Falcetti, Lysenko and Sanfey, 'Reforms and growth in transition: re-examining the evidence', EBRD Working Paper, 90, 2005, pp.1-26 (p.2)

[10] Fischer and Sahay and Vegh, 'Stabilization and growth in transition economies: The early experience', IMF Working Paper, 31, 1996, pp.1-33, (p.17)

is already below the threshold does not have any measurable effect. They further argue that every economy probably has its own threshold.[11]

While macroeconomic stability and economic growth seem to go hand in hand, one has to be aware that the causality is not clear. There appears to be a two way relationship between the two as well as between macroeconomic stability and other aspects of transition. For example, Falcetti, Lysenko and Sanfey argue that inflation and deficits are themselves affected by growth.[12] In the same manner Christoffersen and Doyle point out that inflation is also affected by the output gap, just as economic theory suggests. Another argument is that macroeconomic stabilisation only serves as a transmission mechanism because it is a result of functioning institutions and that diverging growth patterns can be explained by these. This point is made by Gerry, Lee and Mickiewiczwho who write that bad governance, via inefficient and low tax collection, leads to inflation and budget deficits and thus to lower growth.[13] However, here too, seems to be a two way relationship. Hartwell argues that stabilisation allows institutions to grow and that institutions and stabilisation progress in parallel.[14] The next section takes a look at how institutions and growth might be related.

The role of institutions

Institutional development in transition is measured by the EBRD transition indicators. This section takes a look at the institutions-growth relationship. Most of the literature reviewed for this essay agrees that progress in transition as measured by an increase in the overall transition score is associated with higher growth. The EBRD's 2008 transition report finds that an improvement of the average EBRD transition score significantly raises growth in the following year. Their estimation shows that increasing the average EBRD score from 3.0 to 3.1 increases GDP growth by 1% in the subsequent year.[15] Falcetti, Lysenko and Sanfey come to a similar conclusion stating that reforms that increase EBRD indicators also increase growth in future periods. They calculate that increasing the overall index by 0.1,

---

[11]European Bank for Reconstruction and Development, 'Transition Report 1999: Ten years of Transition', EBRD Transition Report, 1999, pp. 1-299 (p. 62)

[12]Falcetti, Tatiana Lysenko and Peter Sanfey, 'Reforms and growth in transition: re-examining the evidence', EBRD Working Paper, 90, 2005, pp.1-26 (p.5)

[13]Gerry, Lee and Mickiewicz, 'Governance, Institutions and Growth: empirical lessons from the post-communist transition', in Enrico Marelli and Marcello Signorelli (ed.), Economic Growth and Structural Features of Transition, United Kingdom, Palgrave Macmillian, 2010, pp. 41-60 (pp. 44-45, 55)

[14]Hartwell, Institutional barriers in the transition to market : examining performance and divergence in transition economies, United Kingdom, Palgrave Macmillan Ltd, 2013, p. 205

[15]European Bank for Reconstruction and Development, 'Transition Report 2008: Growth in Transition', EBRD Transition Report, 2008, pp.1-224 (p. 2)

raises growth by 0.46% in the following years.[16] They further show that this strong and positive link persists if different estimation techniques, time spans are used and additional control variables are introduced.[17] Giving weight to these findings are Havrylyshyn and van Rooden. Using a variety of institutional indicators they conclude that differences in institutional development explain up to 5% of the variation in growth rates across the transition region.[18]

Transition in general appears to have a positive effect on growth. However, transition interacts with different aspects of an economy's institutions. This raises the question, which of these are significant in explaining different growth outcomes. Hartwell tries to disentangle institutional development into a subset of institutions and to determine their contribution to growth. His results indicate that democracy, legislative effectiveness, property rights, business freedom and large and small scale privatization have a positive effect on growth.[19] Out of these, property rights seem to have the biggest influence[20], followed by an effective legal framework and executive constraints.[21]However, as with macroeconomic stabilization in the section above, there seems to be a two way relationship here. Higher growth could facilitate faster institutional development and this could lead to further reforms that facilitate more growth. The direction of the relationship is not clear. Camposand Horvath argue that growth and reform could work in a virtuous circle. Reforms initiate growth and growth provides the resources to compensate for negative effects. This in turn initiates more reforms.[22] Further, Campos and Coricelli define transition as a "simultaneous change in economic structures" and that results depend on the interaction of its components. This assumes that institutions and other parts of the transition process, for example liberalisation, influence each other.[23]

---

[16]Falcetti, Lysenko and Sanfey, 'Reforms and growth in transition: re-examining the evidence', EBRD Working Paper, 90, 2005, pp.1-26 (p.8)

[17] Ibid., p. 2

[18] Havrylyshyn and van Rooden, 'Institutions Matter in Transiton, But so do Policies', Comaparative Economic Studies, 45, 2003, pp. 2-24 (p. 17)

[19]Hartwell, Institutional barriers in the transition to market : examining performance and divergence in transition economies, United Kingdom, Palgrave Macmillan Ltd, 2013, p. 161

[20] Ibid., p. 165

[21]Havrylyshyn and van Rooden, 'Institutions Matter in Transiton, But so do Policies', Comaparative Economic Studies, 45, 2003, pp. 2-24 (pp. 17) and
Hartwell, Institutional barriers in the transition to market : examining performance and divergence in transition economies, United Kingdom, Palgrave Macmillan Ltd, 2013, pp. 165, 202

[22]Campos and Horváth, 'Reform redux: Measurement, determinants and growth implications', European Journal of Political Economy, 28, 2012, pp. 227-237 (p. 233)

[23]Campos and Coricelli, 'Growth in Transition: What We Know, What We Don't, and What We Should', William Davidson Working Paper, 470, 2002, pp. 1-71 (p. 58)

Liberalisation policies

One of the most striking differences between a planned and a market economy is the role of prices. While prices play a vital role as the main source of information in the later, their role in a planned economy is of less importance. Price liberalisation can change the role of prices. Economic theory suggests that liberalising prices would lead to an efficient allocation of resources and thus to growth. Heybey and Murell use an index of cumulative liberalization to investigate the growth-liberalisation relationship and conclude that liberalisation appears to have a positive effect on average GDP growth in 1989-94.[24] The EBRD comes to a similar conclusion. According to them, by 1993 countries with liberalised prices experienced on average positive growth rates in subsequent years.[25] Campos and Coricelli highlight that the extent of price liberalisation, as measured by an index of cumulative price liberalization, is of major importance.[26]Citing Havrylyshin and van Rooden, Falcetti, Lysenko and Sanfey even conclude that economic liberalisation is more important than reforming the institutional framework when it comes to fostering growth.[27]

Another part of liberalisation is opening up to trade. The theoretical benefits of trade are well known and occur through the exploitation of comparative advantages and increased market size. The logical conclusion is that opening formerly closed economies would boost their GDP. Berg, Ostry and Zettelmeyer estimate that reducing restrictions on trade prolongs the average period of uninterrupted growth in an economy. These are 3-8 times longer in countries that have liberalised trade as compared to countries that haven't.[28] Further Falcetti, Lysenko and Sanfey claim that free trade opens up channels through which a country can benefit from its trade partners' economic success. This has happened in the enlarged European Union and, to a lesser extent, the CIS.[29] Christoffersen and Doyle make the same argument stating Russia as an example. They estimate the effect of a country's export partners' growth on the country's own growth. Their results show a significant positive effect of

---

[24] Heybey and Murrell, 'The relationship between economic growth and the speed of liberalization during transition', The Journal of Policy Reform, 3, 1999, pp. 121-137 (pp. 125-127)

[25]European Bank for Reconstruction and Development, 'Transition Report 1999: Ten years of Transition', EBRD Transition Report, 1999, pp. 1-299 (p. 64)

[26]Campos and Coricelli, 'Growth in Transition: What We Know, What We Don't, and What We Should', William Davidson Working Paper, 470, 2002, pp. 1-71 (p. 53)

[27]Falcetti, Lysenko and Sanfey, 'Reforms and growth in transition: re-examining the evidence', EBRD Working Paper, 90, 2005, pp.1-26 (p.3)

[28]Berg, Ostry and Zettelmeyer, 'What makes growth sustained?', EBRD Working Paper, 2011, 133, pp. 1-47 (p. 23)

[29] Ibid., p. 8

trade partner growth.[30] However, since the main economic link between CIS countries and Russia are often remittances and not exports, these results could wrongly attribute this effect to trade liberalisation instead of migration. As trade integration aligns their economic cycles, it can also backfire once an economy gets dragged into another countries recession.

There are also studies that suggest that trade liberalisation does not affect growth. For example, Marelli and Signorelli find no correlation between a country's trade openness and its growth performance. They use the trade to GDP ratio as a proxy for openness.[31] However this ratio is an indicator of the level of trade. It includes geographical factors and resource exports which are usually not much affected by trade restrictions. This can distort the picture. There is also again the problem of causality. Growth can be a product of trade openness but can also be the cause of more openness. For example, growing economies could feel less inclined to protect local industries from foreign competition. The 'what came first' question should be less problematic in the next section which looks at initial conditions.

Initial Conditions and Soviet Legacies

When examining the transition countries and their policies one realises that they have different characteristics. Despite having a similar political and economic system, their historical experiences and economic situation at the beginning as well as the end of the Soviet Era were different. The question comes to mind whether these different initial conditions also play a role. At the outset of transition, economies differed in many ways. Among them are the degree of macroeconomic distortion, caused by economic planning, and their level of development, measured for example by GDP per capita. Looking at distortion in Central and Eastern Europe (CEE) and the former Soviet Union (FSU), de Melo, Denizer, Gelb and Tenev argue that a high level of distortion at the beginning of transition should lower growth. This is because the initial "shock" of liberalization is more damaging the more distorted the economy is.[32]They use different indicators to measure distortion including "market memory", the familiarity with market economic institutions which were still present in CEE, while there was no such memory in the FSU and trade as a share of GDP, trade connections with the outside world were stronger in CEE than in the FSU. Further they use repressed inflation and the black market exchange rate premium to measure distortions. They find a negative correlation between growth and these

---

[30]Christoffersen and Doyle, 'From Inflation to Growth: eight years of transition', Economics of Transition, 8 (2), 2000, pp. 421-451 (pp. 434-435)

[31] Marelli and Marcello Signorelli (ed.), Economic Growth and Structural Features of Transition, United Kingdom, Palgrave Macmillian, 2010 pp. 49-50*

[32]de Melo, Cevdet Denizer, Alan Gelb, and Stoyan Tenev, 'Circumstance and Choice: the Role of Initial Conditions and Policies in Transition Economies', for World Bank, 1997, pp.1-84, (p. 17)

indicators.[33] The 1999 EBRD transition report finds a similar correlation between a lower degree of distortion and a smaller drop in output at the beginning of transition.[34]

What about the other measure? The EBRD and de Melo, Denizer, Gelb and Tenev take a look at the impact of initial levels of development. The later use urbanization, per capita income and over-industrialization to indicate development. Maybe somewhat surprisingly they find that higher levels of these are associated with lower growth.[35] The reason for this might be found in the nature of growth and the particularities of the transition region. Growth tends to be higher for low income countries because of a greater potential for technological convergence. In addition, countries like Azerbaijan and Turkmenistan, with low initial levels of development, became fast growing resource exporters during the transition period.[36] It might be helpful to exclude resource exporters and examine how economies perform, taking into account their levels of GDP to gain a clearer picture. Further Popov argues that higher levels of GDP per capita at the beginning of transition also meant higher levels of distortion, thus leading to lower growth rates.[37] There are also studies which suggest that the importance of initial conditions declines over time as transition proceeds.[38]

Conclusion and implications for the future

This essay discusses some of the main drivers of economic growth in transition. It finds that macroeconomic stability, trade and price liberalisation and institutional reforms support growth. This is also true for a high level of macroeconomic distortions but not initial GDP per capita. However all the policies discussed are also themselves influenced by growth as well as by each other. This makes it impossible to argue for some sort of policy sequencing where some reforms are introduced early while some are delayed. This suggests that comprehensive reforms could be the

---

[33] Ibid., p. 12

[34] European Bank for Reconstruction and Development, 'Transition Report 1999: Ten years of Transition', EBRD Transition Report, 1999, pp. 1-299 (pp. 61-62)

[35] de Melo, Denizer, Gelb, and Tenev, 'Circumstance and Choice. the Role of Initial Conditions and Policies in Transition Economies', for World Bank, 1997, pp.1-84, (p. 29)

[36] Roland, Economies in Transition: The Long-Run View, United Kingdom, Palgrave Macmillan Ltd, 2011, p. 224

[37] Popov, 'Shock Therapy versus Gradualism Reconsidered: Lessons from Transition Economies after 15 Years of Reforms', Comparative Economic Studies, 49, 2007, pp. 1-31 (p. 27)

[38] Ibid., p. 28 and Falcetti, Lysenko and Sanfey, 'Reforms and growth in transition: re-examining the evidence', EBRD Working Paper, 90, 2005, pp.1-26 (pp. 11-12)

safest way to transform an economy. Further, all these policies cannot be pursued forever as stabilisation and liberalisation are at some point achieved. Thus, once transformation is achieved, countries will have to look for other sources of economic growth.

Bibliography

Berg, Ostry and Zettelmeyer, 'What makes growth sustained?', EBRD Working Paper, 2011, 133, pp. 1-47

Campos and Coricelli, 'Growth in Transition: What We Know, What We Don't, and What We Should', William Davidson Working Paper, 470, 2002, pp. 1-71

Campos, Horváth, 'Reform redux: Measurement, determinants and growth implications', European Journal of Political Economy, 28, 2012, pp. 227-237

Christoffersen and Doyle, 'From Inflation to Growth: eight years of transition', Economics of Transition, 8 (2), 2000, pp. 421-451

de Melo, Denizer, Gelb, and Tenev, 'Circumstance and Choice: the Role of Initial Conditions and Policies in Transition Economies', for The World Bank, 1997, pp.1-84

European Bank for Reconstruction and Development, 'Transition Report 2008: Growth in Transition', EBRD Transition Report, 2008, pp.1-224

European Bank for Reconstruction and Development, 'Transition Report 1999: Ten years of Transition', EBRD Transition Report, 1999, pp. 1-299

Falcetti, Lysenko and Sanfey, 'Reforms and growth in transition: re-examining the evidence', EBRD Working Paper, 90, 2005, pp.1-26

Fischer and Sahay and Carlos Vegh, 'Stabilization and growth in transition economies: The early experience', IMF Working Paper, 31, 1996, pp.1-33

Hare and Turley(ed.), Handbook of the Economics and Political Economy of Transition, London and New York, Routledge, 2013

Hartwell, Institutional barriers in the transition to market: examining performance and divergence in transition economies, United Kingdom, Palgrave Macmillan Ltd, 2013

Havrylyshyn and van Rooden, 'Institutions Matter in Transiton, But so do Policies', Comaparative Economic Studies, 45, 2003, pp. 2-24

Havrylyshyn, Divergent paths in post-communist transformation: capitalism for all or capitalism for the few?, United Kingdom: Palgrave Macmillan, 2005

Heybey and Murrell, 'The relationship between economic growth and the speed of liberalization during transition', The Journal of Policy Reform, 3, 1999, pp. 121-137

Marelli and Signorelli (ed.), Economic Growth and Structural Features of Transition, United Kingdom, Palgrave Macmillian, 2010

Mickiewicz, Economics of institutional change: Central and Eastern Europe revisited, United Kingdom, Palgrave Macmillan, 2010

Popov, 'Shock Therapy versus Gradualism Reconsidered: Lessons from Transition Economies after 15 Years of Reforms', Comparative Economic Studies, 49, 2007,pp. 1-31

Roland, Economies in Transition: The Long-Run View, United Kingdom, Palgrave Macmillan Ltd, 2011